ENCOURAGEMENT for COUPLES

Lifelong Love & Partnership

compiled by Fritz Newenhuyse and Elizabeth Cody Newenhuyse

Harold Shaw Publishers
Wheaton, Illinois

Copyright © 1993 by Harold Shaw Publishers

Compiled by Fritz Newenhuyse and Elizabeth Cody Newenhuyse

All rights reserved. No part of this book may be reproduced or transmitted in any form or by any means, electronic or mechanical, including photocopying, recording, or any information storage and retrieval system, without written permission from Harold Shaw Publishers, Box 567, Wheaton, Illinois 60189. Printed in the United States of America.

ISBN 0-87788-213-4

Cover photo © 1993 Luci Shaw

97

2

Printed in Colombia.
Impreso en Colombia.

Unless the LORD builds the house,
its builders labor in vain.

Psalm 127:1, NIV

CONTENTS

Grateful acknowledgment is made to the publishers of the Scripture versions, portions of which are quoted in this book, using the following abbreviations:

KJV King James Version
NASB New American Standard
NEB New English Bible
NIV New International Version
NKJV New King James Version
RSV Revised Standard Version
TLB The Living Bible

Portions from:

The *New American Standard Bible*, © 1960, 1962, 1963, 1968, 1971, 1972, 1973, 1975, 1977 by The Lockman Foundation. Used by permission.

The New English Bible, © The Delegates of Oxford University Press and The Syndics of the Cambridge University Press, 1961. Reprinted with permission.

The *Holy Bible, New International Version*. Copyright © 1973, 1978, 1984 International Bible Society. Used by permission of Zondervan Publishing House. All rights reserved.

The New King James Version. Copyright © 1979, 1980, 1982, Thomas Nelson Inc., Publishers.

The *Revised Standard Version of the Bible*, copyright 1946, 1952, 1971 by the Division of Christian Education of the National Council of the Churches of Christ in the USA, and used by permission.

The Living Bible © 1971. Used by permission of Tyndale House Publishers, Inc., Wheaton, IL 60189. All rights reserved.

INTRODUCTION

Marriage is God's idea. He desires husbands and wives to live in harmony, obedient to him and seeking his will in all aspects of their lives. In his Word, he gives couples encouragement, insight, instruction, and models for godly living. May these selections strengthen your marriage and your walk with Christ.

GOD'S GIFT OF MARRIAGE

One of the great similarities between Christianity and marriage is that, for Christians, they both get better as we get older.
Jean A. Rees

The LORD God said, "It is not good for the man to be alone. I will make a helper suitable for him."...

But for Adam no suitable helper was found. So the LORD God caused the man to fall into a deep sleep; and while he was sleeping, he took one of the man's ribs and closed up the place with flesh. Then the LORD God made a woman from the rib he had taken out of the man, and he brought her to the man.

The man said, "This is now bone of my bones and flesh of my flesh; she shall be called 'woman,' for she was taken out of man." For this reason a man will leave his father and mother and be united to his wife, and they will become one flesh.

Genesis 2:18, 20-24, NIV

When men began to multiply on the face of the ground, and daughters were

born to them, the sons of God saw that the daughters of men were fair; and they took to wife such of them as they chose.
Genesis 6:1-2, RSV

A father can give his sons homes and riches, but only the Lord can give them understanding wives.
Proverbs 19:14, TLB

Who can find a capable wife? Her worth is far beyond coral. Her husband's whole trust is in her, and children are not lacking. She repays him with good, not evil, all her life long. . . . Her sons with one accord call her happy; her husband too, and he sings her praises: "Many a woman shows how capable she is; but you excel them all."
Proverbs 31:10-12, 28-29, NEB

Live happily with the woman you love through the fleeting days of life, for

the wife God gives you is your best reward down here for all your earthly toil.
Ecclesiastes 9:9, TLB

Listen! My lover! Look! Here he comes, leaping across the mountains, bounding over the hills. My lover is like a gazelle or a young stag. Look! There he stands behind our wall, gazing through the windows, peering through the lattice. My lover spoke and said to me, "Arise, my darling, my beautiful one, and come with me."
Song of Solomon 2:8-10, NIV

Some Pharisees came to him to test him. They asked, "Is it lawful for a man to divorce his wife for any and every reason?"

"Haven't you read," he replied, "that at the beginning the Creator 'made them male and female,' and

said, 'For this reason a man will leave his father and mother and be united to his wife, and the two will become one flesh'? So they are no longer two, but one. Therefore what God has joined together, let man not separate."
Matthew 19:3-6, NIV

The husband should fulfill his marital duty to his wife, and likewise the wife to her husband. The wife's body does not belong to her alone but also to her husband. In the same way, the husband's body does not belong to him alone but also to his wife.
1 Corinthians 7:3-4, NIV

Marriage should be honored by all, and the marriage bed kept pure, for God will judge the adulterer and all the sexually immoral.
Hebrews 13:4, NIV

PUTTING GOD FIRST

The center of God's will is our only safety.
Betsie ten Boom

Thou shalt have no other gods before me.
Exodus 20:3, KJV

And now, O Israel, what does the LORD your God ask of you but to fear the LORD your God, to walk in all his ways, to love him, to serve the LORD your God with all your heart and with all your soul, and to observe the LORD's commands and decrees that I am giving you today for your own good?
Deuteronomy 10:12-13, NIV

"But if you are unwilling to obey the Lord, then decide today whom you will obey. Will it be the gods of your ancestors beyond the Euphrates or the gods of the Amorites here in this land? But as for me and my family, we will serve the Lord."
Joshua 24:15, TLB

Unless the LORD builds the house, those who build it labor in vain.
Psalm 127:1, RSV

How blessed is everyone who fears the LORD, who walks in His ways. When you shall eat of the fruit of your hands, you will be happy and it will be well with you. Your wife shall be like a fruitful vine, within your house, your children like olive plants around your table. Behold, for thus shall the man be blessed who fears the LORD.
Psalm 128:1-4, NASB

He who fears the LORD has a secure fortress, and for his children it will be a refuge.
Proverbs 14:26, NIV

"Martha, Martha," the Lord answered, "you are worried and upset about

many things, but only one thing is needed. Mary has chosen what is better, and it will not be taken away from her."
Luke 10:41-42, NIV

"In just a little while I will be gone from the world, but I will still be present with you. For I will live again—and you will too. When I come back to life again, you will know that I am in my Father, and you in me, and I in you. The one who obeys me is the one who loves me; and because he loves me, my Father will love him; and I will too, and I will reveal myself to him."
John 14:19-21, TLB

The jailer called for lights, rushed in and fell trembling before Paul and Silas. He then brought them out and asked, "Sirs, what must I do to be saved?"

They replied, "Believe in the Lord Jesus, and you will be saved—you and your household."
Acts 16:29-31, NIV

So we fix our eyes not on what is seen, but on what is unseen. For what is seen is temporary, but what is unseen is eternal.

Now we know that if the earthly tent we live in is destroyed, we have a building from God, an eternal house in heaven, not built by human hands.
2 Corinthians 4:18–5:1, NIV

So then you are no longer strangers and sojourners, but you are fellow citizens with the saints and members of the household of God, built upon the foundation of the apostles and prophets, Christ Jesus himself being the cornerstone . . .
Ephesians 2:19-20, RSV

Behold, I stand at the door and knock; if anyone hears my voice and opens the door, I will come in to him and eat with him, and he with me.
Revelation 3:20, RSV

PUTTING EACH OTHER FIRST

God does not make the other person as I would have made him. He did not give him to me as a brother for me to dominate and control, but in order that I might find above him the Creator.

Dietrich Bonhoeffer

"If someone forces you to go one mile, go with him two miles."
Matthew 5:41, NIV

And they came to Capernaum; and when He was in the house, He began to question them, "What were you discussing on the way?" But they kept silent, for on the way they had discussed with one another which of them was the greatest. And sitting down, He called the twelve and said to them, "If anyone wants to be first, he shall be last of all, and servant of all."
Mark 9:33-35, NASB

"Be merciful, just as your Father is merciful."
Luke 6:36, NIV

"If I then, your Lord and Teacher, have washed your feet, you also ought to wash one another's feet."
John 13:14, RSV

For by the grace given me I say to every one of you: Do not think of yourself more highly than you ought, but rather think of yourself with sober judgment, in accordance with the measure of faith God has given you.
Romans 12:3, NIV

Each of us should please his neighbor for his good, to build him up.
Romans 15:2, NIV

For, dear brothers, you have been given freedom: not freedom to do wrong, but freedom to love and serve each other.
Galatians 5:13, TLB

Bear one another's burdens, and so fulfil the law of Christ.
Galatians 6:2, RSV

Submit to one another out of reverence for Christ.

Wives, submit to your husbands as to the Lord. . . . Husbands, love your wives, just as Christ loved the church and gave himself up for her. . . . Husbands ought to love their wives as their own bodies. He who loves his wife loves himself.
Ephesians 5:21-22, 25, 28, NIV

Let each of you look not only to his own interests, but also to the interests of others. Have this mind among yourselves, which is yours in Christ Jesus, who, though he was in the form of God, did not count equality with God a thing to be grasped, but emptied himself, taking the form of a servant,

being born in the likeness of men. And being found in human form he humbled himself and became obedient unto death, even death on a cross.
Philippians 2:4-8, RSV

LIFELONG COMMITMENT

The sexes were made for each other, and only in the wise and loving union of the two is the fullness of health and duty and happiness to be expected.
William Hall

Be happy, yes, rejoice in the wife of your youth. Let her breasts and tender embrace satisfy you. Let her love alone fill you with delight.
Proverbs 5:18-19, TLB

A cord of three strands is not quickly broken.
Ecclesiastes 4:12, NIV

Another thing you do: You flood the LORD's altar with tears. You weep and wail because he no longer pays attention to your offerings or accepts them with pleasure from your hands. You ask, "Why?" It is because the LORD is acting as the witness between you and the wife of your youth, because you have broken faith with her, though she is your partner, the wife of your marriage covenant.

Has not the LORD made them one? In flesh and spirit they are his. And why one? Because he was seeking godly offspring. So guard yourself in your spirit, and do not break faith with the wife of your youth.

"I hate divorce," says the LORD God of Israel, "and I hate a man's covering himself with violence as well as with his garment," says the LORD Almighty.
Malachi 2:13-16, NIV

"And it was said, 'Whoever divorces his wife, let him give her a certificate of dismissal'; but I say to you that everyone who divorces his wife, except for the cause of unchastity, makes her commit adultery; and whoever marries a divorced woman commits adultery."
Matthew 5:31-32, NASB

To the married I give this command (not I, but the Lord): A wife must not separate from her husband. But if she

does, she must remain unmarried or else be reconciled to her husband. And a husband must not divorce his wife.
1 Corinthians 7:10-11, NIV

But if the unbeliever leaves [a marriage], let him do so. A believing man or woman is not bound in such circumstances; God has called us to live in peace. How do you know, wife, whether you will save your husband? Or, how do you know, husband, whether you will save your wife?
1 Corinthians 7: 15-16, NIV

SEXUAL FIDELITY

There is a tendency to think of sex as something degrading; it is not. It is magnificent, an enormous privilege, but because of that the rules are tremendously strict and severe.
Francis Devas

Thou shalt not commit adultery.
Exodus 20:14, KJV

Thou shalt not covet thy neighbor's wife.
Exodus 20:17, KJV

Listen to me, young men, and not only listen but obey; don't let your desires get out of hand; don't let yourself think about [an adulteress]. Don't go near her; stay away from where she walks, lest she tempt you and seduce you. For she has been the ruin of multitudes—a vast host of men have been her victims. If you want to find the road to hell, look for her house.
Proverbs 7:24-27, TLB

"You have heard that it was said, 'You shall not commit adultery.' But I say to you that every one who looks at a

woman lustfully has already committed adultery with her in his heart."
Matthew 5:27-28, RSV

Flee from sexual immorality. All other sins a man commits are outside his body, but he who sins sexually sins against his own body. Do you not know that your body is a temple of the Holy Spirit, who is in you, whom you have received from God? You are not your own; you were bought at a price. Therefore honor God with your body.
1 Corinthians 6:18-20, NIV

CHRISTIAN CHARACTER

The Christian goal is not the outward and literal imitation of Jesus, but the living out of the Christ life implanted by the Holy Spirit.
D. W. Lambert

How I long for your precepts! Preserve my life in your righteousness.
Psalm 119:40, NIV

Do not be conformed to this world but be transformed by the renewal of your mind, that you may prove what is the will of God, what is good and acceptable and perfect.
Romans 12:2, RSV

Therefore let him who thinks he stands take heed lest he fall. No temptation has overtaken you but such as is common to man; and God is faithful, who will not allow you to be tempted beyond what you are able, but with the temptation will provide the way of escape also, that you may be able to endure it.
1 Corinthians 10:12-13, NASB

Do not be misled: "Bad company corrupts good character."
1 Corinthians 15:33, NIV

I have been crucified with Christ and I no longer live, but Christ lives in me. The life I live in the body, I live by faith in the Son of God, who loved me and gave himself for me.
Galatians 2:20, NIV

But the fruit of the Spirit is love, joy, peace, patience, kindness, goodness, faithfulness, gentleness, self-control; against such there is no law.
Galatians 5:22-23, RSV

Finally, my brethren, be strong in the Lord, and in the power of his might. Put on the whole armor of God, that ye may be able to stand against the wiles of the devil.
Ephesians 6:10-11, KJV

And this I pray, that your love may abound yet more and more in knowledge and in all judgment; that ye may approve things that are excellent; that ye may be sincere and without offense till the day of Christ; being filled with the fruits of righteousness, which are by Jesus Christ, unto the glory and praise of God.
Philippians 1:9-11, KJV

Finally, brethren, whatever is true, whatever is honorable, whatever is just, whatever is pure, whatever is lovely, whatever is gracious, if there is any excellence, if there is anything worthy of praise, think about these things.
Philippians 4:8, RSV

Therefore, as God's chosen people, holy and dearly loved, clothe yourselves with compassion, kind-

ness, humility, gentleness and patience.
Colossians 3:12, NIV

Obey God because you are his children; don't slip back into your old ways—doing evil because you knew no better. But be holy now in everything you do, just as the Lord is holy, who invited you to be his child. He himself has said, "You must be holy, for I am holy."
1 Peter 1:14-16, TLB

But the wisdom that is from above is first pure, then peaceable, gentle, willing to yield, full of mercy and good fruits, without partiality and without hypocrisy.
James 3:17, NKJV

For if you wander beyond the teaching of Christ, you will leave God behind; while if you are loyal to Christ's teachings, you will have God too. Then you will have both the Father and the Son.

If anyone comes to teach you, and he doesn't believe what Christ taught, don't even invite him into your home. Don't encourage him in any way. If you do, you will be a partner with him in his wickedness.

2 John 1:9-10, TLB

CHRISTIAN LIVING

We talk a great deal of religion in this country, but we need to stop long enough to let our feet catch up with our mouths.
Billy Graham

Be joyful in hope, patient in affliction, faithful in prayer. Share with God's people who are in need. Practice hospitality.
Romans 12:12-13, NIV

Let us behave decently, as in the daytime, not in orgies and drunkenness, not in sexual immorality and debauchery, not in dissension and jealousy. Rather, clothe yourselves with the Lord Jesus Christ, and do not think about how to gratify the desires of the sinful nature.
Romans 13:13-14, NIV

Here I want to add some suggestions of my own. These are not direct commands from the Lord, but they seem right to me: If a Christian has a wife who is not a Christian, but she wants to stay with him anyway, he must not leave her or divorce her. And if a

Christian woman has a husband who isn't a Christian, and he wants her to stay with him, she must not leave him. For perhaps the husband who isn't a Christian may become a Christian with the help of his Christian wife. And the wife who isn't a Christian may become a Christian with the help of her Christian husband. Otherwise, if the family separates, the children might never come to know the Lord; whereas a united family may, in God's plan, result in the children's salvation.
1 Corinthians 7:12-14, TLB

Brothers, if someone is caught in a sin, you who are spiritual should restore him gently. But watch yourself, or you also may be tempted.
Galatians 6:1, NIV

For we are God's workmanship, created in Christ Jesus to do good works,

which God prepared in advance for us to do.
Ephesians 2:10, NIV

Don't be weary in prayer; keep at it; watch for God's answers, and remember to be thankful when they come.
Colossians 4:2, TLB

See that none of you repays evil for evil, but always seek to do good to one another and to all. Rejoice always, pray constantly, give thanks in all circumstances; for this is the will of God in Christ Jesus for you.
1 Thessalonians 5:15-18, RSV

But as for you, teach what befits sound doctrine. . . . and so train the young women to love their husbands and children, to be sensible, chaste, domestic, kind, and submissive to their husbands, that the word of God may not be discredited. Likewise urge the younger men to control themselves. . . .

For the grace of God has appeared for the salvation of all men, training us to renounce irreligion and worldly passions, and to live sober, upright, and godly lives in this world, awaiting our blessed hope, the appearing of the glory of our great God and Savior Jesus Christ, who gave himself for us to redeem us from all iniquity and to purify for himself a people of his own who are zealous for good deeds.
Titus 2:1, 4-6, 11-14, RSV

Do not forget to entertain strangers, for by so doing some people have entertained angels without knowing it.
Hebrews 13:2, NIV

HEALTHY RELATIONSHIPS

The way from God to a human heart
is through a human heart.
S. D. Gordon

"Do not seek revenge or bear a grudge against one of your people, but love your neighbor as yourself. I am the Lord."
Leviticus 19:18, NIV

Behold, how good and pleasant it is when brothers dwell in unity!
Psalm 133:1, RSV

A kindhearted woman gains respect, but ruthless men gain only wealth.

A kind man benefits himself, but a cruel man brings trouble on himself.
Proverbs 11:16-17, NIV

A soft answer turns away wrath, but a harsh word stirs up anger.
Proverbs 15:1, NKJV

Better is a dry morsel with quietness, than a house full of feasting with strife.
Proverbs 17:1, NKJV

Timely advice is as lovely as golden apples in a silver basket.
Proverbs 25:11, TLB

"Blessed are the peacemakers, for they shall be called sons of God."
Matthew 5:9, RSV

Jesus called the crowd to him and said, "Listen and understand. What goes into a man's mouth does not make him 'unclean,' but what comes out of his mouth, that is what makes him 'unclean.' "
Matthew 15:10, NIV

Then Peter came to him and asked, "Sir, how often should I forgive a brother who sins against me? Seven times?"

"No!" Jesus replied, "seventy times seven!"
Matthew 18:21-22, TLB

"In your anger do not sin": Do not let the sun go down while you are still angry, and do not give the devil a foothold. . . .

Do not let any unwholesome talk come out of your mouths, but only what is helpful for building others up according to their needs, that it may benefit those who listen. And do not grieve the Holy Spirit of God, with whom you were sealed for the day of redemption. Get rid of all bitterness, rage and anger, brawling and slander, along with every form of malice. Be kind and compassionate to one another, forgiving each other, just as in Christ God forgave you.

Ephesians 4:26-27, 29-32, NIV

Let your conversation be always full of grace, seasoned with salt, so that you may know how to answer everyone.

Colossians 4:6, NIV

So then, my beloved brethren, let every man be swift to hear, slow to speak, slow to wrath; for the wrath of man does not produce the righteousness of God.
James 1:19-20, NKJV

For every kind of beast and bird, of reptile and creature of the sea, is tamed and has been tamed by mankind. But no man can tame the tongue. It is an unruly evil, full of deadly poison.
James 3:7-8, NKJV

And the harvest of righteousness is sown in peace by those who make peace.
James 3:18, RSV

Do not repay evil with evil or insult with insult, but with blessing, because to this you were called so that you may inherit a blessing.
1 Peter 3:9, NIV

GOD'S PROVISIONS

God has two dwellings—one in heaven and the other in a thankful heart.
Izaak Walton

"'If you follow my decrees and are careful to obey my commands, I will send you rain in its season, and the ground will yield its crops and the trees of the field their fruit.'"
Leviticus 26:3-4, NIV

The Lord himself is my inheritance, my prize. He is my food and drink, my highest joy! He guards all that is mine. He sees that I am given pleasant brooks and meadows as my share! What a wonderful inheritance!
Psalm 16:5-6, TLB

The Lord lifts the fallen and those bent beneath their loads. The eyes of all mankind look up to you for help; you give them their food as they need it. You constantly satisfy the hunger and thirst of every living thing.
Psalm 145:14-16, TLB

The LORD will guide you continually,
And satisfy your soul in drought,
And strengthen your bones;
You shall be like a watered garden,
And like a spring of water,
whose waters do not fail.
Isaiah 58:11, NKJV

"So do not worry, saying, 'What shall we eat?' or 'What shall we drink?' or 'What shall we wear?' For the pagans run after all these things, and your heavenly Father knows that you need them. But seek first his kingdom and his righteousness, and all these things will be given to you as well. Therefore do not worry about tomorrow, for tomorrow will worry about itself. Each day has enough trouble of its own."
Matthew 6:31-34, NIV

"Which of you, if his son asks for bread, will give him a stone? Or if he asks for

a fish, will give him a snake? If you, then, though you are evil, know how to give good gifts to your children, how much more will your Father in heaven give good gifts to those who ask him!"
Matthew 7:9-11, NIV

Now He who supplies seed to the sower and bread for food, will supply and multiply your seed for sowing and increase the harvest of your righteousness; you will be enriched in everything for all liberality, which through us is producing thanksgiving to God.
2 Corinthians 9:10-11, NASB

But godliness with contentment is great gain. For we brought nothing into this world, and it is certain we can carry nothing out. And having food and raiment let us be therewith content.
1 Timothy 6:6-8, KJV

Every good gift and every perfect gift is from above, and cometh down from the Father of lights, with whom is no variableness, neither shadow of turning.

James 1:17, KJV

GOD'S GIFT OF FAMILY

A happy family is but an earlier heaven.
John Bowring

Deeply moved at the sight of his brother, Joseph hurried out and looked for a place to weep. He went into his private room and wept there.
Genesis 43:30, NIV

So Boaz took Ruth and she became his wife. Then he went to her, and the LORD enabled her to conceive, and she gave birth to a son. The women said to Naomi, "Praise be to the LORD, who this day has not left you without a kinsman-redeemer. May he become famous throughout Israel! He will renew your life and sustain you in your old age. For your daughter-in-law, who loves you and who is better to you than seven sons, has given him birth."
Ruth 4:13-15, NIV

Then David turned to Solomon and said:

". . . Solomon, my son, get to know the God of your fathers. Worship and serve him with a clean heart and a willing mind, for the Lord sees every heart and understands and knows every thought."
1 Chronicles 28:8-9, TLB

After Job had prayed for his friends, the LORD made him prosperous again and gave him twice as much as he had before. All his brothers and sisters and everyone who had known him before came and ate with him in his house. They comforted and consoled him over all the trouble the LORD had brought upon him, and each one gave him a piece of silver and a gold ring . . . . [Job] also had seven sons and three daughters. The first daughter he named Jemimah, the second Keziah and the third Keren-Happuch. No-

where in all the land were there found women as beautiful as Job's daughters, and their father granted them an inheritance along with their brothers.
Job 42:10-11, 13-15, NIV

A father of the fatherless, a defender
of widows,
Is God in His holy habitation.
God sets the solitary in families;
He brings out those who are
bound into prosperity;
But the rebellious dwell in a dry land.
Psalm 68:5-6, NKJV

Behold, children are a heritage
from the LORD,
The fruit of the womb is a reward.
Like arrows in the hand of a warrior,
So are the children of one's youth.
Happy is the man who has his
quiver full of them;

They shall not be ashamed,
But shall speak with their
  enemies in the gate.
Psalm 127:3-5, NKJV

And taking a child, He set him before them, and taking him in His arms, He said to them, "Whoever receives one child like this in My name receives Me; and whoever receives Me does not receive Me, but Him who sent Me."
Mark 9:36-37, NASB

"The older brother was angry and wouldn't go in. His father came out and begged him, but he replied, 'All these years I've worked hard for you and never once refused to do a single thing you told me to; and in all that time you never gave me even one young goat for a feast with my friends. Yet when this son of yours comes back after spending your money on prostitutes, you celebrate by killing the finest calf we have on the place.'

" 'Look, dear son,' his father said to him, 'you and I are very close, and everything I have is yours. But it is right to celebrate. For he is your brother; and he was dead and has come back to life! He was lost and is found!' "
Luke 15:28-32, TLB

Near the cross of Jesus stood his mother, his mother's sister, Mary the wife of Clopas, and Mary Magdalene. When Jesus saw his mother there, and the disciple whom he loved standing nearby, he said to his mother, "Dear woman, here is your son," and to the disciple, "Here is your mother." From that time on, this disciple took her into his home.
John 19:25-27, NIV

Now the overseer must be above reproach, the husband of but one wife, temperate, self-controlled, respectable, hospitable, able to teach, not given to drunkenness, not violent but gentle, not quarrelsome, not a lover of money. He must manage his own family well and see that his children obey him with proper respect. (If anyone does not know how to manage his own family, how can he take care of God's church?)

1 Timothy 3:2-5, NIV

HUSBANDS AND WIVES IN THE BIBLE

Marriage is not merely a cultural invention, but God's perfect design for companionship.

R. Paul and Gail Stevens

The Lord visited Sarah as he had said, and the Lord did to Sarah as he had promised. And Sarah conceived, and bore Abraham a son in his old age at the time of which God had spoken to him. . . . Abraham was a hundred years old when his son Isaac was born to him. And Sarah said, "God has made laughter for me; every one who hears will laugh over me." And she said, "Who would have said to Abraham that Sarah would suckle children? Yet I have borne him a son in his old age."
Genesis 21:1-7, RSV

Now Laban had two daughters, Leah, the older, and her younger sister, Rachel. Leah had lovely eyes, but Rachel was shapely, and in every way a beauty. Well, Jacob was in love with Rachel. So he told her father, "I'll work for you seven years if you'll give me Rachel as my wife."

"Agreed!" Laban replied. "I'd rather give her to you than to someone outside the family."

So Jacob spent the next seven years working to pay for Rachel. But they seemed to him but a few days, he was so much in love.

Genesis 29:16-20, TLB

Then Saul gave him his daughter Michal in marriage.

When Saul realized that the LORD was with David and that his daughter Michal loved David, Saul became still more afraid of him, and he remained his enemy the rest of his days. . . .

Saul sent men to David's house to watch it and to kill him in the morning. But Michal, David's wife, warned him, "If you don't run for your life tonight, tomorrow you'll be killed." So Michal let David down through a window, and he fled and escaped. Then

Michal took an idol and laid it on the bed, covering it with a garment and putting some goats' hair at the head.

When Saul sent the men to capture David, Michal said, "He is ill."

1 Samuel 18:27-29; 19:11-14, NIV

The Lord said to me, "Go, show your love to your wife again, though she is loved by another and is an adulteress. Love her as the LORD loves the Israelites, though they turn to other gods and love the sacred raisin cakes."

So I bought her for fifteen shekels of silver and about a homer and a lethek of barley. Then I told her, "You are to live with me many days; you must not be a prostitute or be intimate with any man, and I will live with you."

For the Israelites will live many days without king or prince, without sacrifice or sacred stones, without ephod

or idol. Afterward the Israelites will return and seek the LORD their God and David their king. They will come trembling to the LORD and to his blessings in the last days.
Hosea 3, NIV

Now the birth of Jesus Christ took place in this way. When his mother Mary had been betrothed to Joseph, before they came together she was found to be with child of the Holy Spirit; and her husband Joseph, being a just man and unwilling to put her to shame, resolved to divorce her quietly. But as he considered this, behold, an angel of the Lord appeared to him in a dream, saying, "Joseph, son of David, do not fear to take Mary your wife, for that which is conceived in her is of the Holy Spirit; she will bear a son, and you shall call his name

Jesus, for he will save his people from their sins."

. . . When Joseph woke from sleep, he did as the angel of the Lord commanded him; he took his wife, but knew her not until she had borne a son; and he called his name Jesus.
Matthew 1:18-21, 24-25, RSV

In the days of Herod, king of Judea, there was a priest named Zechariah, of the division of Abijah; and he had a wife of the daughters of Aaron, and her name was Elizabeth. And they were both righteous before God, walking in all the commandments and ordinances of the Lord blameless. But they had no child, because Elizabeth was barren, and both were advanced in years.

Now while he was serving as priest before God when his division was on duty . . . there appeared to him an

angel of the Lord standing on the right side of the altar of incense. And Zechariah was troubled when he saw him, and fear fell upon him. But the angel said to him, "Do not be afraid, Zechariah, for your prayer is heard, and your wife Elizabeth will bear you a son, and you shall call his name John."
Luke 1:5-8, 11-13, RSV

Greet Priscilla and Aquila, my fellow workers in Christ Jesus, who risked their own necks for my life, to whom not only I give thanks, but also all the churches of the Gentiles. Likewise greet the church that is in their house.
Romans 16:3-5, NKJV

COMFORT IN TIMES OF STRUGGLE

As sure as ever God puts his children in the furnace he will be in the furnace with them.
C. H. Spurgeon

Yea, though I walk through the valley of the shadow of death, I will fear no evil: for thou art with me; thy rod and thy staff they comfort me.
Psalm 23:4, KJV

God is our refuge and strength, a very present help in trouble. Therefore will not we fear, though the earth be removed, and though the mountains be carried into the midst of the sea . . .

The LORD of hosts is with us; the God of Jacob is our refuge.
Psalm 46:1-2, 7, KJV

Do you not know? Have you not heard? The LORD is the everlasting God, the Creator of the ends of the earth. He will not grow tired or weary, and his understanding no one can fathom. He gives strength to the weary and increases the power of the weak. Even youths grow tired and weary, and

young men stumble and fall; but those who hope in the LORD will renew their strength. They will soar on wings like eagles; they will run and not grow weary, they will walk and not be faint.
Isaiah 40:28-31, NIV

"Can a mother forget the baby at her breast and have no compassion on the child she has borne? Though she may forget, I will not forget you!"
Isaiah 49:15, NIV

"Those who mourn are fortunate! for they shall be comforted."
Matthew 5:4, TLB

"Let not your hearts be troubled; believe in God, believe also in me. In my Father's house are many rooms; if it were not so, would I have told you that I go to prepare a place for you? And when I go and prepare a place for

you, I will come again and will take you to myself, that where I am you may be also."
John 14:1-3, RSV

"Peace I leave with you; my peace I give you. I do not give to you as the world gives. Do not let your hearts be troubled and do not be afraid."
John 14:27, NIV

Therefore, since we have been justified through faith, we have peace with God through our Lord Jesus Christ, through whom we have gained access by faith into this grace in which we now stand. And we rejoice in the hope of the glory of God. Not only so, but we also rejoice in our sufferings, because we know that suffering produces perseverance; perseverance, character; and character, hope. And hope does not disappoint us, because God has poured out his love into our hearts by the Holy Spirit, whom he has given us.

Romans 5:1-5, NIV

And we know that all that happens to us is working for our good if we love God and are fitting into his plans. . . .

What can we ever say to such wonderful things as these? If God is on our side, who can ever be against us? Since he did not spare even his own Son for us but gave him up for us all, won't he also surely give us everything else? . . .

For I am convinced that nothing can ever separate us from his love. Death can't, and life can't. The angels won't, and all the powers of hell itself cannot keep God's love away. Our fears for today, our worries about tomorrow, or where we are—high above the sky, or in the deepest ocean—nothing

will ever be able to separate us from the love of God demonstrated by our Lord Jesus Christ when he died for us.
Romans 8:28, 31-32, 38-39, TLB

Praise be to the God and Father of our Lord Jesus Christ, the Father of compassion and the God of all comfort, who comforts us in all our troubles, so that we can comfort those in any trouble with the comfort we ourselves have received from God.
2 Corinthians 1:3-4, NIV

May our Lord Jesus Christ himself and God our Father, who loved us and by his grace gave us eternal encouragement and good hope, encourage your hearts and strengthen you in every good deed and word.
2 Thessalonians 2:16-17, NIV

Therefore, since we have a great high priest who has gone through the heavens, Jesus the Son of God, let us hold firmly to the faith we profess. For we do not have a high priest who is unable to sympathize with our weaknesses, but we have one who has been tempted in every way, just as we are—yet was without sin. Let us then approach the throne of grace with confidence, so that we may receive mercy and find grace to help us in our time of need.

Hebrews 4:14-16, NIV

LOVE

There is no surprise more wonderful than the surprise of being loved; it is God's finger on humanity's shoulder.
Charles Morgan

"This is My commandment, that you love one another, just as I have loved you."
John 15:12, NASB

Knowledge puffs up, but love builds up.
1 Corinthians 8:1, NIV

Though I speak with the tongues of men and of angels, but have not love, I have become sounding brass or a clanging cymbal. And though I have the gift of prophecy, and understand all mysteries and all knowledge, and though I have all faith, so that I could remove mountains, but have not love, I am nothing. And though I bestow all my goods to feed the poor, and though I give my body to be burned, but have not love, it profits me nothing.

Love suffers long and is kind; love does not envy; love does not parade itself, is not puffed up; does not behave rudely, does not seek its own, is not provoked, thinks no evil; does not rejoice in iniquity, but rejoices in the truth; bears all things, believes all things, hopes all things, endures all things.

Love never fails.

1 Corinthians 13:1-8, NKJV

Be imitators of God, therefore, as dearly loved children and live a life of love, just as Christ loved us and gave himself up for us as a fragrant offering and sacrifice to God.

Ephesians 5:1-2, NIV

And over all these virtues put on love, which binds them all together in perfect unity.

Colossians 3:14, NIV

Above all hold unfailing your love for one another, since love covers a multitude of sins.
1 Peter 4:8, RSV

See how great a love the Father has bestowed upon us, that we should be called children of God; and such we are.
1 John 3:1, NASB

Beloved, let us love one another, for love is from God; and everyone who loves is born of God and knows God. The one who does not love does not know God, for God is love. By this the love of God was manifested in us, that God has sent His only begotten Son into the world so that we might live through him. . . .

And this commandment we have from Him, that the one who loves God should love his brother also.
1 John 4:7-9, 21, NASB